D0288460

the
DISCIPLESHIP
Series

KNOWING

SCRIPTURE

SIX STUDIES FOR GROUPS
OR INDIVIDUALS
WITH NOTES FOR LEADERS

CAROLYN NYSTROM

ZondervanPublishingHouse
Grand Rapids, Michigan

A Division of HarperCollins*Publishers*

Requests for information should be addressed to:
Zondervan Publishing House
Grand Rapids, MI 49530

ISBN 0-310-54721-0

Edited by Jack Kuhatschek
Cover design by Tammy Grabrian Johnson
Cover illustration by Britt Taylor Collins
Interior design by Ann Cherryman

Printed in the United States of America

01 02 03 04 05 / ❖ CH / 12 11 10 9 8

Contents

102533

The Discipleship Series

Welcome to The Discipleship Series, a unique new program designed with one purpose in mind—to make you a stronger, more effective disciple of Jesus Christ.

Whether you are a new Christian, a newly committed Christian, or someone who simply wants a deeper walk with God, The Discipleship Series can help you reach your goal of spiritual maturity.

You'll be learning from people who are known for their wisdom and godly example. The authors of this series are not armchair theologians, but seasoned veterans who have been disciples and disciplemakers for many years. Step by step they will guide you through the essentials of what it means to follow Christ and to become more like him.

The Discipleship Series is designed to be flexible. You can use the guides in any order that is best for you or your group. They are ideal for Sunday-school classes, small groups, one-on-one relationships, or as materials for your quiet times.

Because each guide contains only six studies, you can easily explore more than one facet of discipleship. In a Sunday-school class, any two guides can be combined for a quarter (twelve weeks), or the entire series can be covered in a year.

Each study deliberately focuses on a limited number of passages, usually only one or two. That allows you to see each passage in its context, avoiding the temptation of prooftexting and the frustration of "Bible hopscotch" (jumping from verse to verse). If you would like to look up additional passages, a Bible concordance will give the most help.

The Discipleship Series helps you *discover* what the Bible says rather than simply *telling* you the answers. The questions encourage you to think and to explore options rather than merely to fill in the blanks with one-word answers.

Leader's notes are provided in the back of each guide. They show how to lead a group discussion, provide additional information on questions, and suggest ways to deal with problems that may come up in the discussion. With such helps, someone with little or no experience can lead an effective study.

Suggestions for Individual Study

1. Begin each study with prayer. Ask God to help you understand the passage and to apply it to your life.

2. A good modern translation, such as the *New International Version,* the *New American Standard Bible,* or the *New Revised Standard Version,* will give you the most help. Questions in this guide, however, are based on the *New International Version.*

3. Read and reread the passage(s). You must know what the passage says before you can understand what it means and how it applies to you.

4. Write your answers in the space provided in the study guide. This will help you to clearly express your understanding of the passage.

5. Keep a Bible dictionary handy. Use it to look up any unfamiliar words, names, or places.

Suggestions for Group Study

1. Come to the study prepared. Careful preparation will greatly enrich your time in group discussion.

2. Be willing to join in the discussion. The leader of the group will not be lecturing but will encourage people to discuss what they have learned in the passage. Plan to share what God has taught you in your individual study.

3. Stick to the passage being studied. Base your answers on the verses being discussed rather than on outside authorities such as commentaries or your favorite author or speaker.

4. Try to be sensitive to the other members of the group. Listen attentively when they speak, and be affirming whenever you can. This will encourage more hesitant members of the group to participate.

5. Be careful not to dominate the discussion. By all means participate! But allow others to have equal time.

6. If you are the discussion leader, you will find additional suggestions and helpful ideas in the leader's notes at the back of the guide.

Introducing Knowing Scripture

A sturdy sunburned woman squats on a dirt floor, writing pad and pencil in hand, tape recorder churning. A bare-breasted mother sits nearby on a string hammock nursing her baby—and talking. Children, some dark, some blonde, play a game of pebbles along dirt paths. They talk too—the blond child more fluently than his mother. Handmade booklets with pencil sketches and simple sentences line a nearby shelf. Bible translation is in process.

Wycliffe Bible Translators works worldwide in hundreds of settings like these. WBT estimates that 300 million people have no Scripture in their own language. Indeed, many of these people have *nothing* written in their language. Theirs is a language for speaking, and it is the language of their thoughts. Six thousand Wycliffe staff members try to solve this problem. They are among the most adventurous and creative Christians alive. They pack up their children and portable belongings, and fly, cart, or hike into the most remote areas of the world.

There they adopt the clothing, food, housing and many customs of the people. They dispense medicine, bandage wounds, teach nutrition and agriculture—and listen.

They also write. Starting with oral tapes, they progress to invented alphabet, to hand-constructed reading primers, to literacy classes, to patiently translated paragraphs of the Scripture, to printed booklets one biblical book at a time, finally to a finished product: all of Scripture in the people's own language.

Why? For those of us who can purchase a Bible in almost any town with the money earned from an hour of work, it is hard to comprehend the cost of a Bible translator's work. Yet that work testifies to the value of Scripture—God's written revelation of himself. Without that written Word, our knowledge of God would be limited to oral testimony, observation of God's creation, and personal experience. While these latter three are powerful magnets to God, magnets that God has used throughout history to draw people to himself, they lack the orderly explanation of who God is and what he expects of his people. This comes from Scripture alone.

Because the Bible is such an extraordinary book, it is important that we know some basic facts about it. The Scriptures are composed of two volumes, called the Old and New Testaments. The Old Testament consists of thirty-nine books, written by almost as many authors, over a thousand-year period from 1400 B.C. to 400 B.C. (dates of writing widely accepted by conservative scholars). The New Testament contains twenty-seven books composed in the last half of the first century A.D. (again by conservative estimates).

Some Christian groups also include twelve apocryphal Old Testament books, but even those who consider these disputed books as part of their Scripture believe them to be more important to history than to faith.

The sixty-six (or seventy-eight) books range over a variety of literary genres. There are letters, poems, statistics, laws (moral and civil), prayers, sermons, parables, historical accounts, stories, teachings, prophecies, and even a grief journal—aptly named Lamentations.

How and when were these books put together, and who decided what ancient writings to include? During the time of Christ, the Old Testament was already in place and was considered sacred by Jews of his day. In fact, the New Testament helps to establish the authority of the Old Testament by quoting from it some six hundred times. Many of these quotations come from Christ himself.

The New Testament, which was completed by the end of the first century, came into immediate use by the early church. But it was not until a council meeting of church fathers at Carthage in A.D. 397 that a total list of "approved" books was established. That list remained constant for a thousand years.

While 350 years after Christ's death may seem a long time before establishing which New Testament books were "holy," the criteria used clearly reveal why those books were acknowledged and others rejected. The Carthage council chose books that had (1) apostolic authorship or authentication, (2) Christ-honoring doctrinal content, and (3) continuous acceptance and fruitful use within the church.

As for authenticity (how we know that what we read in our Bible really comes from an ancient text), archaeologists have recovered some 5,366 partial or complete Greek manuscripts of New Testament books—many dating from the first century. That number is far greater than for any other ancient text.

The Bible itself has much to say about its source and value. Many passages touch those subjects, but the Apostle Paul's letter to the young pastor Timothy is most concise. He writes in 2 Timothy 3:16: "All Scripture is God-breathed and is useful for teaching, rebuking, correcting and training in righteousness, so that the man of God may be thoroughly equipped for every good work."

So we, who follow Jesus, should be passionate about Scripture. Why? Because by knowing Scripture we come to know and love the God who has redeemed us and who has given us this gift of his own words.

What should we expect to happen as a result of our study? We may be tempted to study Scripture because of what we can "get out of it." But a more careful look at Paul's letter to Timothy points to a different motive. We should instead be looking forward to what Scripture is doing *in* us. The Bible, rightly used, will teach, rebuke, correct, and train us to be righteous. Drastic work, for those of us who prefer moral leisure! Yet if we learn to read it, understand it, and apply it, God's Word will change us. And that change will make us more and more like the person God has designed us to be.

May it be so for all who use this guide.

Carolyn Nystrom

Psalm 19
2 Timothy 3:14–17

Why Study Scripture?

My childhood Bible, now lying open on top of my current study Bible, tells its own story. It speaks of a child growing up in a home and church that valued Scripture. The inscription reads, "Presented to Miss Carolyn Mae Abbott, age 10, by Mother and Daddy." Its frayed and ripped pages shout, "Sword Drill." Hash marks next to 365 references state, "Read the Bible through in a year"—year after year. Its spotted edges speak of frequent dashes through Ohio rain without protection of coat or umbrella. Its broken binding and torn black cover edges decree, "Economy first." Its fine-printed King James text without grace of interpretative commentary says, "Go to the 'original' and figure it out for yourself." It's a well-worn Bible carried from home to church to school and back until I finished high school. (I think I graduated to a red-letter edition when I headed for college.)

But the clippings and penciled notes inside speak not just of the text, but of me, the person I was in those growing years. I seem to have tucked symbols of myself inside those tissue pages. A lesson outline for a backyard Bible club—far too long and wordy for wriggly farm children, sitting in the hot sun on straight-backed chairs dragged from our living room. A penciled note during a sermon: "Can you come Tuesday night?" A phone number (no name) and only five digits. Neatly penned prospective colleges: Asbury, Moody, Bryan, Wheaton. A song from a church solo (mine?): "In life or death—and life is surely flying, / The crib and coffin carved from the selfsame tree ..." I couldn't have understood those cryptic words then, but the imagery startles me now that I have lived through the simultaneous deaths of my daughter and her unborn child. Various penciled sayings-to-live-by, most now trite in my mind, but one that has become more true with the years: "Only one life, will soon be past / Only what's done for Christ will last."

I've worn out a half dozen Bibles since that first one. They speak of stages of my life. Some I've misused, some I've ignored, some I've used well. One (a favorite) I lost. The Bible is God's Word—written. I suppose I've always known that. Not a typical child's view, I know. But the pages of my first Bible stand as witness.

---

1. What are some of your early memories of the Bible?

---

2. Read Psalm 19. Notice the natural divisions in this psalm. What title would you give to each section?

3. Repetition of similar ideas often gives clues to the emphasis of a passage. What words and phrases indicate that the heavens *speak* to us about God (vv. 1–6)?

4. What can you discover about the *message* spoken by the heavens? (For example: What is the message? To whom is it spoken? When is it given?)

5. Many societies worship the moon, or the stars, or the sun. How does this psalm define a proper place in the universe for these heavenly bodies?

6. Consider, for a moment, that when you praise God, the moon, and sun, and stars praise God with you. How might this affect your worship?

7. In verses 7–11, David moves from what the heavens reveal about God to what his written Word reveals. What adjectives (such as "perfect") does David use to describe God's written communication?

8. Notice the action phrases in these verses (such as *reviving* the soul"). What all does God's written Word do for us?

9. Which of the benefits of Scripture make you more eager to spend time in God's Word? Why?

10. As we read and meditate on Scripture, why do we need the Lord's help (vv. 12–14)?

11. Read 2 Timothy 3:14–17. How did Timothy benefit from being taught the Scriptures as a child (vv. 14–15)?

12. Many people believe that the Bible is excellent human literature, full of interesting stories and teachings. Why, according to Paul, is this an inadequate view (vv. 16–17)?

13. As you look at the various uses of Scripture (vv. 16–17), what do you discover about your needs as a Christian?

14. How might a regular time of Bible study and meditation help to meet those needs?

Memory Verse

All Scripture is God-breathed and is useful for teaching, rebuking, correcting and training in righteousness, so that the man of God may be thoroughly equipped for every good work.

2 Timothy 3:16

Between Studies

Use this week to survey the Bible. Page through its sixty-six books, taking time to dip in and read a story here, a few pages there, a song, a poem, a letter. The outline below may help.

❑ The first five books of the Old Testament are often called "The Law." They include the accounts of Creation and early civilization. Two good samples to read are Genesis 1–3 and Exodus 19–20.

❑ The books of history run from Joshua through Esther. Read the book of Ruth, an engaging short story of the era.

❑ Poetry appears from Job through the Song of Songs. Select one or two psalms, the third chapter of Ecclesiastes, and the first chapter of the Song of Songs for reading.

❑ The Old Testament ends with five long books of prophecy and twelve short ones. The short book of Habakkuk is a good sample to read.

❑ The New Testament begins with four gospels, each one an account of Christ's birth, life, and death. Pick out something that intrigues you and read it. Let it help you *know* Jesus.

❑ Acts is an account of the founding of the early church. Scan it, noticing key people, places, and events.

❑ Romans is a detailed written explanation of the Christian faith to the believers in Rome. Scan it now, but come back later for a more thorough study.

- ❏ Corinthians through Thessalonians are Paul's letters to specific churches he founded. Pick one of the shorter letters, and read it as if Paul sent it to your own church.
- ❏ Timothy and Titus are Paul's letters to pastors. Page through their practical advice.
- ❏ Philemon is a letter to the Christian owner of a runaway slave who has become a Christian.
- ❏ Hebrews describes the Christian faith from the perspective of an Old Testament scholar.
- ❏ James through Jude are called general letters, because they seem addressed to all Christians. Notice the emphasis on love in 1 John.
- ❏ Revelation is a mysterious book of prophecy. To put your present life into perspective, end your survey of the Scriptures by reading aloud the last two chapters of the Bible.

Habakkuk

Getting an Overview

Are you a person who "can't see the forest because of the trees"? Do you get lost examining the veins of a leaf, the striations of bark, the outline of limbs, but never quite get the general contours of hills and streams and floor and canopy that say "forest"?

The same thing happens in Bible study. We can get stuck on phrase-by-phrase, verse-by-verse reading, picking apart how this subject relates to that verb, untying a sticky theological knot here and there, and totally miss the big picture of what God is communicating through the general sweep of a book. In so doing, we may even misunderstand the smaller ideas we think we have grasped. After all, a mushroom and an acorn look a little alike—except that one lives on the forest floor and the other grows on a tree.

Many techniques can help you gain an overview of a book before you dig in for serious study. A "read-aloud-at-one-sitting" approach is a good way to start.

As you read, notice the tone or mood of the book. Is it joyful? Sorrowful? Angry? Filled with praise?

What kind of literature is it: story, teaching, letter, poetry, prophecy?

Next look for such clues as the major characters, major events, or major themes in the book.

Watch, too, for hints about the writer and his audience. What problems are they facing? What questions have they asked? What are their primary concerns? How does the writer respond to each of these?

An early trip through a book is a good time to note your own questions: "What questions does this book raise in my mind?" "What sections are hard for me to understand?" "What emotions does it arouse in me?" "How might I grow from a study of this book?"

Today's study will use some of these techniques to create an overview of one of Scripture's less-studied books. This lesson is not intended as an in-depth study of "veins" and "bark." Instead, it looks for "contours" and "streams." It is a way to begin study. And good work, at the overview stage, will help prevent the mushroom/acorn mistake.

Habakkuk is a three-chapter book—one of the small books of Old Testament prophecy. In it, Habakkuk complained to God. And God responded.

1. If you could have a "gripe session" with God, what would you complain about?

2. Read the book of Habakkuk, noticing who is speaking in each major section. What title would you give to each section that summarizes its content?

3. What do the tone and structure of this book tell you about Habakkuk and his people?

4. How would you summarize in one sentence Habakkuk's first major complaint against God (1:1–4)?

5. Habakkuk's first complaint was about his own people, yet God responded by talking about their enemies, the Babylonians (vv. 5–11). As God described the Babylonians, what words and phrases would inspire fear?

6. Reread Habakkuk's second speech to God (vv. 12–2:1) in the tone of voice you think he would have used. What is the gist of his second complaint against God?

7. In chapter 2, God responds to Habakkuk's second complaint by telling him how other nations will eventually taunt Babylon. Notice the repeated use of the word "woe" that forms an outline for the chapter. What, in God's view, had Babylon done wrong, and what was the corresponding judgment against each of those wrongs?

8. In chapter 3, Habakkuk recalls God's powerful deeds during Israel's exodus from Egypt. When he comes to verse 16, he expresses both fear and trust. What would lead to that combination of trusting fear (vv. 1–15)?

9. Habakkuk 3:17 speaks of a loss that would be devastating in an agricultural society. What would represent a similar devastating loss to you?

10. Meditate on the words of verses 18–19. How is Habakkuk's description of God appropriate in view of the losses he is about to face?

11. How might this record of Habakkuk's dialogue with God help you if you were to experience a loss like his?

Memory Verse

Though the fig tree does not bud and there are no grapes on the vines, though the olive crop fails and the fields produce no food, though there are no sheep in the pen and no cattle in the stalls, yet I will rejoice in the LORD, I will be joyful in God my Savior. The Sovereign LORD is my strength; he makes my feet like the feet of a deer, he enables me to go on the heights.

Habakkuk 3:17–19

Between Studies

Do an overview study of the book of Jonah. Begin by reading through the entire book in one sitting. As you read, try to discover the main theme of the book. Think of a brief title that will summarize that theme.

Next, find the major divisions in the book. As you reread those sections, look for their main subject, and then think of a title that will summarize each one.

You might also want to look for logical relationships between the sections or divisions. How does each section relate to the one that comes before and after? (For example, why is Jonah willing to obey God in chapter 3, when he was unwilling in chapter 1? Chapter 2 provides the answer.)

Finally, draw a horizontal chart that will visually record your findings.

1 Kings 18:16–19:18

Looking for Details

God is a good writer. Sure, God used human messengers when he conveyed Scripture in its original form. And God used human theologians in the third century to decide just which books should appear in the canon. And God used human editors and linguists to translate the Scripture from its ancient Hebrew and Greek into today's modern languages. Yet, when today's writer studies Scripture, she finds a remarkably good script.

Journalists, for example, often calculate the quality of their writing by a simple measure called the Ramsey Score. Sacramento English teacher George Ramsey developed this scale in an attempt to help his students cut the mush out of their writing and practice precision. He told them to evaluate their papers by assigning one point for each mention of four items: a proper name, a numeral, a direct quotation, or an illustration or example.

By this standard, narrative sections of the Scripture stand well indeed. They are full of the specific details that we expect in a credible newspaper account. A reader of Scripture gets the immediate impression that the person who reported the event saw and heard what happened—and that he had an eye for detail.

Details are important to writers and readers alike. Details answer the questions: Who? What? Where? When? How much? They take a story away from the realm of opinion and into verifiable fact. They establish a writer's credibility. William Strunk, Jr., author with E. B. White of a small handbook, The Elements of Style *(an almost universal tool for writers), says in his rule #12, "Use definite, specific, concrete language." It is these "definite, specific, concrete" details that make a story come alive in a reader's mind.*

Here, too, Biblical narrative excels. We see a widow so poor that she has only two copper coins. But she gives them both to God (Luke 21). We see Joseph given a many-colored coat by his father, dumped into a well near Dothan by his eleven brothers, and then sold for twenty silver shekels to Ishmaelite spice traders on the way from Gilead to Egypt (Genesis 37). If we lived in that era, we could verify the facts on the details alone.

Any honest approach to Scripture involves, at first, a careful survey of details. And narrative passages, in particular, spread those details throughout the text.

Today you will study an encounter between the Hebrew prophet Elijah, Queen Jezebel, and God. Its attention to details is worthy of any of today's best newspapers.

---

1. If you were reading a newspaper account of a fire, what details would you expect to find?

---

2. Read 1 Kings 18:16–46. What details stand out in your mind as adding color and drama to this story?

3. Select a five- or six-verse section from this chapter and calculate a Ramsey Score (see p. 26). What do these details contribute to your understanding of what happened?

4. Notice as many names of people and places as you can in the text. What do these names tell you about the two opposing sides? about the distances involved? (Check a map.)

5. Look for as many numbers as you can find in this passage. What do they tell you about the strength of the two opposing sides?

6. Survey the passage again looking for quotations. Who is speaking in each case, and to whom?

7. What can you learn about Elijah's character by the way he handled his conversations?

8. If you had been one of the people who witnessed these events, what would you think of Elijah's God? Why?

9. Read 1 Kings 19:1–18. What significance do numerical details play in this account? (Check a map again.)

10. What do Elijah's words reveal about the depth of his discouragement?

11. In what different ways did God deal with Elijah's depression?

12. Why do you think God appeared to Elijah the way that he did (vv. 11–13)?

13. Why might the people who witnessed God's work on Mount Carmel be surprised at the way he dealt with the discouraged Elijah?

14. Which of God's qualities, as you have observed them in these two chapters, would you like to see at work in a situation you are facing?

Memory Verse

"Then you call on the name of your god, and I will call on the name of the LORD. The god who answers by fire—he is God." . . . Then the fire of the LORD fell and burned up the sacrifice, the wood, the stones and the soil, and also licked up the water in the trench. When all the people saw this, they fell prostrate and cried, "The LORD—he is God! The LORD—he is God!"

1 Kings 18:24, 38–39

Between Studies

Read Acts 1:1–11. As you read, look for such details as: *Who* is mentioned in the text (author, readers, characters)? *What* is happening (actions, events, repeated words)? *Where* is it taking place (consult a Bible atlas)? *When* does it happen (days, weeks, months, years)? *Why* is it happening (reasons, explanations)? *How* is the passage written (type of literature, how it is organized, figures of speech). Bombard the passage with as many questions as you can think of.

Record your findings so that you can refer to them later.

Matthew 19:16–26

Discovering
Meaning

"God doesn't want me to fly," quips Key Biscayne radio
pastor Steve Brown, in defending his queasiness about air-
planes. "The Bible proves it. It says, 'Lo, I am with you
always.' God wants me to stay low!"

No one, however, takes Steve or his quote seriously—not
even Steve. He grits his teeth and climbs on the plane. And
when he teaches from the Bible (seriously, that is) he uses logical steps for discovering its meaning.

A variety of techniques can keep us from making Steve's
kind of mistake. Most of them follow the same steps and principles that any literature student would use.

1. Context provides major clues to meaning. Consider first
the literary context. Reading the paragraphs or chapters
before and after the passage will give you a better grasp of the
author's message.

Consider next the historical context. Try to understand
the questions, problems, and concerns of the original readers
and how the author speaks to those issues.

2. A paragraph is the basic unit of thought. (Except for
poetry, in which case we think in stanzas.) Reading and thinking by paragraphs may seem a little clumsy at first because of
verse markings. But verse numbers and paragraph breaks
were added by editors long after the original manuscripts were
formed. As you read a paragraph, try to discover the main subject being discussed.

3. Grammar gives additional hints about meaning. Did the writer suddenly change tenses, from past to present, from present to future? This can indicate a shift in meaning. Is the author asking questions, giving commands, making statements? Each of these details can clarify the meaning of a passage.

4. Scripture is internally consistent. That means that Scripture does not disagree with itself. While no one claims to understand every verse in the Bible, we can reject any interpretation that contradicts the clear teaching of Scripture as a whole. It also means that Scripture is its own best commentary. Other passages, especially on related themes by the same author, will often shed light on the passage we are studying.

5. Reference books can be helpful tools for clarifying the passage or book we are studying. Bible dictionaries can explain the meaning of unfamiliar words, places, and people in the Bible. Atlases focus on the geography of Bible lands. Concordances list all the occurrences of the words in the Bible. Commentaries explain the background and meaning of a passage or book.

Today's study focuses on finding accurate meaning in a passage of Scripture. You will use most of the techniques mentioned above.

---

1. What are some of the motives people have for trying to do good?

2. Read Matthew 19:16–26. Do you think the rich man was trying to earn his salvation ("What good thing must *I do* to get eternal life?"), or was he merely seeking salvation? Explain.

3. What, if anything, is surprising about Christ's response: "If you want to enter life, obey the commandments" (v. 17)?

Why do you think Jesus points the man to the Law rather than to faith?

4. Scripture is often its own best commentary. Which of the ten commandments does Jesus include, and which does he omit (see Exodus 20:1–17)?

5. How do the first four of the ten commandments differ from the ones Jesus mentions?

6. Jesus also mentions one of the two greatest commandments (v. 19). Which one does he omit (see Matthew 22:34–40)?

7. Why do you think Jesus only mentions the commandments related to neighbors and omits those that focus on the man's relationship with God?

8. The rich man is obviously self-confident (v. 20). How does Christ's statement in verse 21 expose the man's true condition (v. 22)?

9. By clinging to his wealth, how had the rich man broken not only the tenth commandment (see Exodus 20:17) but also the first two (see also Paul's comments on greed in Colossians 3:5)?

10. Context can clarify the meaning of a passage. How does the rich man's self-confident attitude differ from that of the little children (Matthew 19:13–15)?

11. Reference books can also be helpful tools for interpreting a passage. *The Expositor's Bible Commentary* on Matthew states: "Most Jews expected the rich to inherit eternal life, not because their wealth could buy their way in, but because their wealth testified to the blessing of the Lord on their lives." How does this clarify the disciples' astonishment at Christ's statements about the rich (vv. 23–26)?

12. Wealth is not the only idol we can worship. What idols threaten to claim first place in your life?

13. What would it take for you to renounce those idols in order to better follow Jesus?

Memory Verse

When the disciples heard this, they were greatly astonished and asked, "Who then can be saved?"

Jesus looked at them and said, "With man this is impossible, but with God all things are possible."

Matthew 19:25–26

Between Studies

This week do an in-depth study of the meaning of Christ's rather mysterious statements in Matthew 19:28. If possible, consult various translations, related passages (see Genesis 49:1–28; Luke 22:24–30, 66–71; Mark 16:19–20; Philippians 2:5–11; Revelation 4; 7:1–8; 20:4–6), and a Bible dictionary. At the conclusion of your study, you may also wish to consult a commentary on Matthew or a one-volume Bible commentary.

Try to resolve the following questions:

❑ What does Jesus mean by the "renewal of all things"?
❑ Who are the "you" who will sit on the twelve thrones?
❑ When and where will the scene occur?
❑ What kind of judgment will the people on the twelve thrones perform?
❑ Who are the twelve tribes of Israel?
❑ Will sitting on one of the twelve thrones be a privilege? A responsibility? Or both? Explain.
❑ How does the meaning you have discovered in this verse relate to the conversation in the text surrounding it? (If it doesn't fit, consider other meanings.)

Matthew 22:34–40
James 1:16–25

Learning to Apply

Several years ago some seminary students were asked to prepare and deliver a sermon on the parable of the Good Samaritan. (In that parable Jesus condemned religious leaders for not helping an injured man beside the road.) At the appointed time for each seminarian, just as he headed for class to preach his sermon, someone posing as a "needy person" tried to stop him and ask for help. Not one of them stopped. Not one of them helped. After all, they had a sermon to preach!

Something had gone wrong with their Bible study. Each student learned the facts. He learned the meaning. He prepared to communicate clearly what he had learned. The Scripture entered his eyes, churned around in his brain, and came out of his mouth. But it never penetrated his heart.

As Christians, we need to take the Bible not only as a guide for thinking, but also as a guide for living. Yet there are appropriate and inappropriate ways to do this.

One clue for discovering how to apply the Bible is found in Christ's Great Commandment (Matthew 22:34–40). Religious Jews of his day had cataloged all of Old Testament moral teaching and had come up with 613 commands from God.

These commands covered everything from worshiping God to dealing with mold and mildew.

Some of the commands seemed small; others were of major importance. Some seemed bound by a single cultural era; others seemed universal. Some laws seemed to conflict with other laws. So the religious lawyers presented Christ with a thought-provoking question: Which is the most important law?

Christ's reply gave them (and us) profound insight into what God expects from his people. And with that reply, we can begin to move Scripture from our heads to our hearts.

In the previous three studies you worked primarily on head knowledge. You learned how to see an overview of a book, how to pick apart a passage for details, and how to correctly find its meaning. Today's study assumes a basic knowledge of those earlier steps. Most of today's questions focus on, "So what?" "How are you going to live differently?"

---

1. When you try to live out what Scripture teaches, what problems do you encounter?

---

2. Read Matthew 22:34–40. This great command, or "perfect law," is divided into two parts. Why is it hard for you to love God in the way this command describes?

3. What is hard about loving others with the same intensity that we love ourselves?

4. If "all the Law and the Prophets hang on these two commandments," why do you think the other biblical commands were necessary?

5. How is application easier if we realize that all the specific commands of Scripture reflect broader principles, such as loving God and our neighbor?

6. Read James 1:16–25. James says that every good and perfect gift comes from God (vv. 17–18). What do you appreciate about your heavenly Father and what he has given you?

7. Verses 19 and 20 speak of the dangers of anger. How can being quick to listen and slow to speak help control anger?

8. In what settings do you most need that kind of strategy for anger-control?

9. Verse 21 introduces other pressures against a righteous life. What pressures toward "moral filth and evil" are common in your surroundings?

10. How can humbly accepting the word planted in you (v. 21) help you resist those forces?

11. James urges us to take God's word seriously (vv. 22–25). What motives might a person have for becoming knowledgeable about the Scriptures?

12. Twice James warns about being deceived (vv. 16, 22). What is dangerous about studying the Scriptures but not acting on what you find there?

13. What, according to verse 25, are we to do with God's "perfect law"?

14. James compares Scripture to a mirror (vv. 23–24). How is looking in a mirror similar to looking into Scripture?

15. What practical steps can you take so that Scripture can perform the best functions of a mirror in your life?

Memory Verse

Do not merely listen to the word, and so deceive your-selves. Do what it says. Anyone who listens to the word but does not do what it says is like a man who looks at his face in a mirror and, after looking at himself, goes away and immedi-ately forgets what he looks like.

James 1:22–24

Between Studies

This week study Luke 6:20–49, sometimes called Christ's "Sermon on the Plain." It is a section of the moral teachings that Jesus presented to his disciples. Use the following outline to record your work.

❑ Heading: Copy Matthew 22:37–38 as a guide to help you interpret the meaning of Christ's various com-mands.

❑ Content: Write each principle or command from the Luke 6 passage. Below each statement from the text, write one way that you could begin to let that command touch your life. (Be as specific and practical as possi-ble.)

❑ Conclusion: Copy James 1:25 as encouragement to let these Scriptures continue to work in your life.

Psalm 139

Praying
the
Scriptures

For two years, during the midsection of our marriage, my husband and I were foster parents. We had requested newborn, preadoptive infants. I love babies, and I figured if they were quickly going into good adoptive homes, I wouldn't have too much trouble giving them up.

We had only one preadoptive infant during those two years—and we only had him for a weekend. What we did have was a long array of children who had been physically and emotionally abused. We saw children of alcoholics and drug addicts. We saw broken arms and legs and heads (on infants!). We saw malnutrition. We saw sexual abuse—on a preschooler. We saw a teenage mother who so grieved about "giving away" her baby that she thought maybe she should get pregnant again. All of these children slept in our beds, ate at our table, visited our pediatrician, attended our church. And all of them (except for the two we adopted) went back home.

I learned to pray. Sure, I had prayed before—prayers of thanks, praise, intercession for friends, and the usual "gimme" prayers. But now I prayed in earnest out of a sense of need: the needs of my children and the needs of myself.

Of course, I took appropriate actions to meet those needs. I wiped noses, bandaged scrapes, rocked to sleep, comforted *nightmares, went to court (over and over), and pleaded with caseworkers to follow the least harmful route within the law for "my" kids. But in the end, there was little I could control of the future. So at nap time, on warm days, I tucked the kids into bed, climbed the hill behind our house, leaned my back against the bark of a century-old oak tree, and prayed. I could still hear and see any major disturbance in the house below, but with that restriction, it was my private time of conversation with God.*

Sometimes I did not know what to say, so I just sat quietly and listened to birds and insects and the flutter of breeze in the leaves above. And I knew that God sat there with me. Sometimes, lacking words of my own, I turned to the Scriptures and prayed those words to God, attaching footnotes from my own setting as they came to my mind.

I think I learned more about prayer during those two years of foster care than I had at any previous stage of my life. I came to God in need, and he taught me to worship him.

Norwegian theologian, O. Hallesby, in his devotional classic Prayer *wrote, "Prayer is for the helpless . . . To pray is to open the door unto Jesus and admit Him into your distress. Your helplessness is the very thing which opens wide the door unto Him and gives Him access to all your needs."*

Some people learn to pray during times of thanksgiving, or during times of forgiveness, or during times of praise. But for me it was a time of need that grew my prayers. And when I looked to the Scriptures, I found (through the biblical prayers) that others had been there ahead of me.

---

1. During what time in your life has prayer been particularly important?

2. Read Psalm 139. This psalm is a prayer of worship. What lines express your own appreciation of God?

3. In the first stanza (vv. 1–6), David repeats the word "know" or "knowledge." What all does he say that God knows?

4. How do you feel about God knowing you in the way that this stanza describes?

5. David begins the second stanza (vv. 7–12) with the idea of God's presence. Why might the presence of God, as it is described here, be both a threat and a comfort?

6. Have you ever wanted to hide from God? Explain.

7. Stanza 3 (vv. 13–16) speaks of God as Creator. What statements here show the extent of God's care for you as an individual?

8. Meditate for a moment on the words of verse 16. How can the words here affect the way you feel about your life—and your death?

9. Stanza 4 (vv. 17–18) forms a summary of the poem thus far and a bridge into the next section. How might this stanza help you to love or appreciate God?

10. Stanza 5 (vv. 19–22) appears on the surface not to fit with the rest of the prayer. In view of what David has been meditating about God, why might he feel particularly harsh toward the wicked at this point?

11. In stanza 6 (vv. 23–24), David wants to be sure that he is not among those he condemned in stanza 5. How does his description of God up to this point add importance to what he now asks of God?

12. Why might it be hard to pray this section of David's prayer?

13. Psalm 139 is a prayer of worship. Many prayers of Scripture also include prayers of petition. We may use them to pray for people we care about. Read aloud each of the prayers listed below. After each prayer say, "Lord, I (we) pray this prayer for . . . and then add the name or names of those for whom you make this request.

- ❑ Romans 15:13
- ❑ 2 Corinthians 13:7
- ❑ Ephesians 3:16–21
- ❑ 1 Thessalonians 5:23
- ❑ Philemon 4–7
- ❑ Hebrews 13:20–21

Memory Verse

Search me, O God, and know my heart; test me and know my anxious thoughts. See if there is any offensive way in me, and lead me in the way everlasting.

Psalm 139:23–24

Between Studies

Each day this week select a different prayer from the previous list. Personalize the prayer by inserting a name and making minor changes in the pronouns. Then pray the prayer aloud for that person.

Leader's Notes

Leading a Bible discussion—especially for the first time—can make you feel both nervous and excited. If you are nervous, realize that you are in good company. Many biblical leaders, such as Moses, Joshua, and the apostle Paul, felt nervous and inadequate to lead others (see, for example, 1 Corinthians 2:3). Yet God's grace was sufficient for them, just as it will be for you.

Some excitement is also natural. Your leadership is a gift to the others in the group. Keep in mind, however, that other group members also share responsibility for the group. Your role is simply to stimulate discussion by asking questions and encouraging people to respond. The suggestions listed below can help you to be an effective leader.

Preparing to Lead

1. Ask God to help you understand and apply the passage to your own life. Unless that happens, you will not be prepared to lead others.

2. Carefully work through each question in the study guide. Meditate and reflect on the passage as you formulate your answers.

3. Familiarize yourself with the leader's notes for the study. These will help you understand the purpose of the study and will provide valuable information about the questions in the study.

4. Pray for the various members of the group. Ask God to use these studies to make you better disciples of Jesus Christ.

5. Before the first meeting, make sure each person has a study guide. Encourage them to prepare beforehand for each study.

Leading the Study

1. Begin the study on time. If people realize that the study begins on schedule, they will work harder to arrive on time.

2. At the beginning of your first time together, explain that these studies are designed to be discussions, not lectures. Encourage everyone to participate, but realize that some may be hesitant to speak during the first few sessions.

3. Read the introductory paragraph at the beginning of the discussion. This will orient the group to the passage being studied.

4. Read the passage aloud. You may choose to do this yourself, or you might ask for volunteers.

5. The questions in the guide are designed to be used just as they are written. If you wish, you may simply read each one aloud to the group. Or you may prefer to express them in your own words. Unnecessary rewording of the questions, however, is not recommended.

6. Don't be afraid of silence. People in the group may need time to think before responding.

7. Avoid answering your own questions. If necessary, rephrase a question until it is clearly understood. Even an eager group will quickly become passive and silent if they think the leader will do most of the talking.

8. Encourage more than one answer to each question. Ask, "What do the rest of you think?" or "Anyone else?" until several people have had a chance to respond.

9. Try to be affirming whenever possible. Let people know you appreciate their insights into the passage.

10. Never reject an answer. If it is clearly wrong, ask, "Which verse led you to that conclusion?" Or let the group handle the problem by asking them what they think about the question.

11. Avoid going off on tangents. If people wander off course, gently bring them back to the passage being considered.

12. Conclude your time together with conversational prayer. Ask God to help you apply those things that you learned in the study.

13. End on time. This will be easier if you control the pace of the discussion by not spending too much time on some questions or too little on others.

Many more suggestions and helps are found in the book *Leading Bible Discussions* (InterVarsity Press). Reading it would be well worth your time.

Study One   Why Study Scripture?

Psalm 19; 2 Timothy 3:14–17

Purpose: To understand the importance Scripture places on God's written Word.

Question 1.

Every study begins with an "approach question," which is discussed *before* reading the passage. An approach question is designed to do three things.

First, it helps to break the ice. Because an approach question doesn't require any knowledge of the passage or any special preparation, it can get people talking and can help them to warm up to each other.

Second, an approach question can motivate people to study the passage at hand. At the beginning of the study, people in the group aren't necessarily ready to jump into the world of the Bible. Their minds may be on other things (their kids, a problem at work, an upcoming meeting) that have nothing to do with the study. An approach question can capture their interest and draw them into the discussion by raising important issues related to the study. The question becomes a bridge between their personal lives and the answers found in Scripture.

Third, a good approach question can reveal where people's thoughts or feelings need to be transformed by Scripture. That is why it is important to ask the approach question *before* reading the passage. The passage might inhibit the spontaneous, honest answers people might have given, because they feel compelled to give biblical answers. The approach question allows them to compare their personal thoughts and feelings with what they later discover in Scripture.

As you begin today's study, allow several people to speak of their early experiences with the Bible. A little humor won't hurt. Be aware that, for some, "early" may mean the present.

Question 2.
Accept any reasonable divisions and titles. Use the question to examine the general topics of the psalm. The questions in this study provide one way to divide the psalm.

Question 3.
Your group should point out such words as "declare," "proclaim," "speech," "knowledge," "language," "voice," "heard," and "words."

Question 5.
These verses give great respect to the heavenly bodies. Verses 4 and 5 speak of the sun as a "bridegroom," and a "champion," but it is *God* who has made the sky a tent for the sun. Verses 2–4 speak of the far-reaching, continuous flow of communication from the heavenly bodies. But verse 1 says that it is God's glory (not their own) that they proclaim.

Question 7.
Look for such words and phrases as "perfect," "trustworthy," "right," "radiant," "pure," "sure," "righteous," "more precious than gold," "sweeter than honey."

Question 8.
Pick out the verb phrases in the passage. Your group should cite such words as "reviving," "making wise," "giving joy," "giving light," "enduring," "warned."

Question 11.
Use this question to study the details of this passage in Paul's letter to Timothy.

Question 14.
Help your group begin to set some goals for their response to Scripture and for the use of this study guide.

For those who are new to the Bible or who want a quick refresher, point out the Between Studies section as a good place to start.

Study Two   Getting an Overview
Habakkuk

Purpose: To use a variety of Bible study techniques to survey the book of Habakkuk.

Question 1.
Try to involve each person in the group with this question. If some people feel that this kind of question is inappropriate, remind them of how honest the authors of Scripture were with God—particularly in the Psalms.

Question 2.
You will be able to answer this question best if you divide the reading according to the following sections. This will give

the feeling of dialogue as the text constructs it: Habakkuk 1:1–4; 1:5–11; 1:12–2:1; 2:2–20; 3:1–15; 3:16–19.

Don't worry if section titles are not precisely in line with the content. At this point in the study, people should be getting a general feel for the book. More exact understanding will emerge as the study progresses.

Question 3.

Answers here should reflect the entire book. The colorful language of the book shows that Habakkuk is a fine poet with deep faith in God. The people he addresses have a long history as God's people, yet he sees them as fallen away from following godly precepts. Habakkuk believes that he can communicate with God and that God responds to him. He shows profound respect for God. At this stage, your group may want to point out some of the more colorful (and often quoted) statements of the book. Among them: Habakkuk 2:2; 2:4; 2:14; 2:20; 3:2; 3:17–19. Notice also Habakkuk's names for God and how they reflect his faith. (See Habakkuk 1:12 and 3:18–19.)

Question 4.

The gist of Habakkuk's complaint is that his people have turned from God and become wicked—and God hasn't done anything about it. Verse 3 says, "Why do you tolerate wrong?" In the words of verse 4, "The wicked hem in the righteous, so that justice is perverted."

Question 5.

Your group should point out a variety of phrases from Habakkuk 1:5–11.

Question 6.

Allow a few moments for people to scan Habakkuk 1:12–2:1. Then ask a fluent reader to interpret the passage with his or her voice. When Habakkuk learns that God is going to use the Babylonians as instruments to bring judgment on his own people, Habakkuk complains again. The words of verse 13 express in summary, "Why are you silent while the wicked swallow up those more righteous than themselves?"

Question 7.
Use this question to study each of the five "woes" of chapter 2. Notice the complaint and the corresponding judgment of each. Then discuss how the complaint and judgment relate to each other.

Question 8.
Use this question to survey the details of Habakkuk 3:1–15.

Question 10.
Study Habakkuk's names for God and what each one says about his character. You may also add Habakkuk's names for God in 1:12. Habakkuk says a great deal about his faith by the way he addresses God. He also says a great deal about God.

Question 11.
Refer to some of the feared losses of question 9. Encourage thoughtful, honest response.

Study Three   Looking for Details
1 Kings 18:16–19:18

Purpose: To learn how to spot details and to see how they contribute to the total impact of a passage of Scripture.

Question 2.
Group members should mention details that stand out in their minds at this point. A more thorough examination of the passage will come in later questions.

Question 3.
Divide the passage into paragraphs, ask each person to rate one paragraph, and then have each one give a one sen-

tence report of his or her findings. The report should include a Ramsey Score and a sentence about how those details contributed to understanding. If the group is large, work in pairs. (No need to cover the entire passage; a few sample paragraphs will be sufficient.)

Question 4.

This passage contains more than sixty proper names. For those who don't mind marking in their Bibles, give the option of circling the names.

Spend a few minutes for observation, and then begin to discuss the two opposing sides that these names reveal. Be prepared to point out places on a map, both in this chapter and in the next one. You'll save group time if you spot and mark the places on the map prior to your meeting.

Question 5.

About a dozen numbers appear in the text. Give people the option of underlining these if they wish. The numbers, too, contribute to a visual picture of the strength of each side. Let your group point these out rather quickly, and then discuss what strengths these numbers convey.

Question 6.

You might want to suggest that people mark each quotation in the margin with the initial of the person or persons speaking. (Don't take too much time with this.) Then discuss how these direct quotations of speech reveal Elijah's character.

Question 7.

Notice particularly the difference in tone and content of Elijah's words as he shifted from Ahab, to the people, to God, to his servant. Each dialogue reveals another side of the speaker. It shows Elijah, but it also reveals his relationship to the person he addresses.

Question 9.

Use similar techniques to those in the previous chapter, but pass over the technique rather quickly and move on to the content that these details reveal.

Question 10.

See verses 4–5, 10, and 14. Notice that in spite of God's personal and strong intervention, Elijah's verbal evaluation of the situation did not change at this point.

Question 11.

God's actions appear in verses 6–9, 11–13, and 15–18. Let the group discuss how these works and words of God might have had an impact on Elijah's needs.

Question 13.

The powerful, angry God of chapter 18, who spoke in fire and storm, moves through chapter 19 as the God who nourishes, feeds, and comforts Elijah and speaks to him in a gentle whisper. Both chapters reveal the character of God. What might the people of Mount Carmel have learned from chapter 19?

Question 14.

Pace your study to allow time for quiet, honest reflection here. Those who are in a pitched battle against evil may wish God to reveal some of his awesome Mount Carmel qualities. Those who feel in need of comfort may prefer the quiet whisper. Anyone who is discouraged may want the detailed help supplied in 19:5–9. God is all of these—and more.

Study Four   Discovering Meaning
Matthew 19:16–26

Purpose: To use a variety of techniques to discover the meaning of Christ's teaching in Matthew 19:16–26.

Question 2.

The Philippian jailer asked Paul and Silas, "What must I do to be saved" (Acts 16:30). In that case, at least, there seems to have been no thought of earning salvation. The rich, young ruler, however, appears to have had such a motive, as the later verses indicate.

Question 3.

If we were teaching a class on evangelism, and someone gave the response Jesus gave, we would fail him on the spot! From the very beginning of our Christian life—and even earlier—we are taught that we cannot receive salvation by keeping the commandments. Salvation is a gift, received by faith.

Obviously, Jesus knew this. Our curiosity should be aroused, therefore, as to why he pointed the man to the Law rather than to faith. Perhaps Jesus felt it was necessary to help the man see his need for salvation before offering it to him.

Question 5.

The first four commandments deal with our relationship with God. The commandments Jesus mentions (five through nine) deal with our relationships with others. The tenth commandment, which Jesus omits, will be discussed in question 9.

Questions 7.

Of course it is impossible to know for certain why Jesus took the approach he did. Yet it seems that he was gradually exposing the man's true spiritual condition rather than making accusations that the man would deny.

First, Jesus deals with the man's relationship to his neighbor (vv. 18–19). Then he focuses on the man's relationship to God (v. 21).

Questions 8–9.

By asking the rich young man to sell his possessions, Jesus was forcing the man to confront his covetousness. Clearly, the man's wealth meant more to him than loving God, following

Jesus, and getting eternal life. Therefore, the man had not only broken the commandment against covetousness but also the commandments related to putting God first and avoiding idolatry.

By asking the man to give his wealth to the poor, Jesus may also have been exposing the shallow nature of the man's relationship to his neighbor.

We should realize that Jesus was not exposing the man's sinfulness in order to humiliate him but to give him a chance to confront his sin and to repent.

Study 5   Learning to Apply
Matthew 22:34–40; James 1:16–25

Purpose: To observe what Scripture says about its applicability to our lives. To discuss how we can begin to live out several concepts addressed in a specific passage.

Question 1.
Discuss general answers about the problems of applying Scripture and actually *doing* anything about it. More specific difficulties in applying a passage of Scripture will come up in later questions.

Questions 2 and 3.
These are difficult commands! Use these questions to help your group examine both parts of the command and to honestly calculate what it would cost to put them into practice.

Jesus said, "All the Law and the Prophets hang on these two commandments." The Law was the first five books of the Old Testament. The Prophets were the remainder of the Old Testament. In other words, the Law and the Prophets are another way of saying, "All of Scripture written to this date."

The Mark account of this same event has a teacher of the law asking Jesus, "Of all the commandments, which is the most important?" Jewish scholars of Christ's era had cataloged all of

59

the biblical laws. They had counted 613 individual commands. No wonder they needed a priority system! Jesus summarized all of these Old Testament laws, and his own modifications of them, with these two commands. We may use this "Great Command" to help us discover what God expects from us.

Question 4.

The other biblical commands were necessary "to define and illustrate the general commands about love in the specific situations of everyday life. For example, what did it mean to love your neighbor in business practices? 'Do not use dishonest standards when measuring length, weight or quantity' (Leviticus 19:35). What did it mean to love those who were hungry and needy? 'When you reap the harvest of your land, do not reap to the very edges of your field or gather the gleanings of your harvest. . . . Leave them for the poor and the alien' (Lev. 19:9–10)" (Jack Kuhatschek, *Taking the Guesswork out of Applying the Bible* [Downers Grove, Ill.: InterVarsity Press, 1990], 53).

Question 5.

"The Bible contains many levels of application. These levels are like a pyramid, with only two commands (love for God and neighbor) at the pinnacle and all other commands at various levels between the pinnacle and the base.

The principles near the top of the pyramid are fewer in number because they are more general and abstract. The commands nearer the base of the pyramid (such as 'Do not muzzle your ox') are more numerous because they are more specific, detailed and concrete.

The commands near the base sometimes seem pointless or obscure until we move up to higher levels on the pyramid to discover the principles or reasons for the commands. Conversely, the principles near the top of the pyramid often seem vague and abstract until they are fleshed out by the more concrete commands near the base. . . .

If we realize that every passage of Scripture is part of the larger biblical pyramid with its various levels, applying the Bible becomes much easier. If a passage appears too specific to apply to our situation, we simply move up a level, looking for a general principle that we can apply" (Kuhatschek, *Applying the Bible,* 54–57).

Question 6.

Your group should discuss what it means that God is described as "Father," that he is Father of the "heavenly lights," that he "does not change" like the shifting shadows that those heavenly lights produce. Verse 18 speaks of God as Creator.

These verses also inform us that "every good and perfect gift" comes from God. Encourage group members to express thanks for some of the good in their lives and to acknowledge that all of those good gifts come from God. If it is appropriate, you may wish to pause at the conclusion of this question in order to thank God for who he is and for what he has given to you.

Verse 18 speaks particularly of one of God's good gifts. He has given us "birth" through the truth of his Word. Our new birth, or salvation through Jesus Christ, comes as a gift from God. Because of that new birth, we belong to him as his "first-fruits."

Question 10.

The terms "humbly accept," "planted in you," and "save" (v. 21) are relevant to this question. If God's Word is so much a part of us that it is planted within us, if it is so important that it leads us to salvation, if we humbly accept that Word as one of God's good gifts to us, then all that we have taken into our inner core is at opposite poles from the evil forces that surround us. Encourage the group to think of some practical ways God's Word helps us to resist evil.

Question 11.

People have a host of reasons for becoming knowledgeable about Scripture. We may wish to enlarge our education. We may want to defend a particular doctrinal position. We may want to be thought of as "religious." We may want to be able to answer other people's questions. We may want the companionship that people who are familiar with Scripture enjoy. We may enjoy the Bible as literature. We may want to learn about religion or about God. We may want to use it to prove that our ideas are right, or that someone else's are wrong. We may want to use Scripture as a text for scholarly study. Or, we may want to let Scripture be a guide for our system of beliefs and for our daily lives.

Question 12.
Self-deceit is hard to spot, especially when it gives us a religious feeling. It is easy for us to feel that we are pleasing God if we are studying Scripture. But biblical knowledge and even Scripture memory do not, by themselves, lead to godly living. So daily reading, memorization programs, and scholarly study (while they are admirable practices) all may lead to self-delusion. We may think we are obeying God when in fact we are merely exercising our minds. To obey God, we must let the Scriptures touch our lives. When it does, it will change our feelings, our thoughts, *and* our actions.

Question 13.
Your group should comment on the terms "looks intently," "continues," "do," and "not forgetting."

Question 15.
Help your group to be as practical and specific as possible here.

Study 6   Praying the Scriptures
Psalm 139

Purpose: To learn to pray biblical prayers of worship and petition.

Question 1.

Listen to several responses to this question. If you want follow-up questions (and have time for them) ask, "What did you learn about prayer at that time? What did you learn about God? About yourself?"

Question 2.

Linger long enough on this question to allow each person to respond. This poem is one of the high points of Old Testament literature. Enjoy it as a whole before beginning a stanza-by-stanza dissection.

Question 3.

This stanza describes God's omniscience. (God is all-knowing.) Examine the details of what that means.

Question 5.

This stanza describes God's omnipresence. (God is present everywhere. He is not limited by time and space.) Be sure that your group discusses both the comfort and the threat of that attribute of God.

Question 10.

After such a vivid picture of God's might and his love, to be an enemy of God is unthinkable to David. Compared to the brightness of God's glory, those who are wicked seem blacker than ever. To the extent that David places himself in God's camp, he sees God's enemies as his own.

Question 13.

Assign each person present to read one of the prayers and the closing line that begins, "Lord, we pray this for . . ." Then pause and allow each person the chance to say the first name of one or more people. When the names have ceased for one prayer, go on to the next one. Close the time of biblical prayers with a simple benediction.